Shipping Container Homes

A Complete Guide to Building a Container Home and Tiny House Living

Peter Johnson

Table of Contents

Introduction 1
Chapter 1: The Benefits of Tiny Living 5
Chapter 2: The Building Process 21
Chapter 3: What's Tiny Home Living Like? 38
Conclusion 48
References 50

Introduction

I don't know about you, but my phone says I spend an average of between two and three hours per day on social media.

With little interest in posting myself, most of my time is spent staring at inspirational stories or photos. Every once in a while, I come across a post regarding container houses, and I simply can't help but click on the link, or double-tap, in the case of Instagram.

These houses represent a dream I'm sure we've all had at a certain point in our lives—a small, cozy house in the middle of nowhere, surrounded by nature. No nosy neighbors, no responsibilities, no noise, and no air pollution. But then reality strikes and you realize that the house you already live in won't pay for itself, so you have to expose yourself to all of the above if you want to keep on living.

But what if you could just have a part of that dream? The cozy little house, surrounded by nature. What if it were you living in that perfectly little shipping container home you saw on Instagram?

We often see things we like and think about doing some research to see if it's viable, but then life happens. We forget about it and move on with life as it is.

But what about life in the "new normal?" I've heard those two words so many times recently that I hate to use them myself, but there's no better way to describe the situation we find ourselves in. The COVID-19 pandemic has changed our lives irrevocably. It's impossible to go back. It has caused too much devastation to the economy and social interaction. We're being forced to explore new avenues for almost everything we had before, including housing.

Even before the pandemic, shipping container housing saw an uptick in interest, mostly thanks to Millennials. It's not hard to see why. It offers a vastly cheaper alternative to traditional housing, but that's something we'll delve deeper into later. For now, you just need to know that shipping container houses offer a lot of bang for the buck.

Millennials caught on early, simply because they live in a world where a starter home is no longer a thing. Thanks to a combination of student loans and the general cost of living, for many, there simply isn't enough money left to pay for a house.

We now live in a world where affordability will remain the number one consideration for people when it comes to most things. Those who already own homes might want to scale down, while those in the market for a home might not want to spend as much as they originally had intended.

The second important reason why people are suddenly interested in shipping container living is the idea that it offers space. Not so much the house itself, but the space around it. It's the complete opposite of the big city lifestyle we used to lust after.

I say "used to" because that's something else the pandemic changed. Looking back at how quickly the COVID-19 virus spread in densely populated cities, I'm willing to bet that a large number of people aren't interested in living that way anymore. Sure, the chances of another pandemic in our lifetime are slim, but it has now happened twice in the last 100 years. If it's not something you thought about before, it most certainly is something you're thinking about now.

Big city life comes with other downsides as well: the constant noise, lack of privacy, pollution, and traffic. The only argument I can think of in favor of city living is that it's where you work, but that's another thing the pandemic changed. It's now blatantly obvious that the nine-to-five, office-bound way of doing things is horribly outdated. Remote working, I think, will become the norm in the coming years. So why still live in the city when there's so much open space out there? Why hasn't somebody thought about this before?

Well, they have. It's just that it's now suddenly the most attractive housing option. Before that, it was a small trend a few people bought into. Before that, it was a practical and cost-effective way of housing.

The abridged version of the history goes something like this: The standardized container was developed to make shipping and transport easier. The USA imports more than it exports, which means there's always a surplus of containers standing around. Since containers were developed to be strong, weather-resistant, and modular, it didn't take someone long to figure out that they could be used as a building material.

The first-ever official record of a shipping container home patent was granted to Phillip Clark in 1987. Yet decades earlier, others had thought to repurpose containers. In 1962 the Insbrandtsen Company filed a patent for using shipping containers as exhibition booths for products (*Shipping Container History*, 2020).

There's also an undocumented history to consider. If you traveled through Africa at any time during the last four decades, you would have noticed shipping containers being used as housing. These aren't the modern shipping container houses we see on Instagram these days, but rather just a basic shipping container with a bed in it. The container was nothing more than a box to keep the weather and wild animals out. In remote places, it was either that or a tent.

This method is still employed today. The last time I saw shipping containers used to house a mass of workers was in 2018 in Lesotho. A new diamond mine was being developed far from any town or city, so the mining company constructed its own tiny city out of shipping containers.

The inventor of the shipping container was a man called Malcolm McLean. He owned a transportation business and could see the desperate need for a standardized shipping container, not just for shipping purposes, but for easier transportation on trucks across the land as well. He was so convinced by his idea, that he sold his transportation business, took out a loan, and bought an existing shipping company with docking rights across the world.

The first ship using his containers left the dock in New Jersey in April 1956. Before it reached its final destination of Houston, McLean already had orders rolling in. His method was 25% cheaper than anything else available at the time, which is a significant percentage in a billion-dollar industry like shipping and transportation.

At that point in time, he likely knew that what he had done would revolutionize an industry. I don't think he knew that one day, just over 60 years later, his invention would revolutionize the housing industry as well...

Chapter 1: The Benefits of Tiny Living

Shortly after my introduction to shipping container houses, I saw an advertisement for a job running a hotel on the coast of Mozambique. The job was sold as the perfect opportunity for someone who wanted to get off the grid and live in paradise. I followed the link and saw the job came with a house, which happened to be two stacked shipping containers. From the outside, it looked a bit shabby and in need of some paint, but otherwise, it was perfectly livable. It had a bed, bathroom, dining area, hammock, and a beautiful view of the ocean.

The idea seemed magnificent, but, like most people, my visions of moving to a remote coastal house on the other side of the world were short-lived.

I first saw a shipping container house up close at a housing expo. It was a magnificent thing, consisting of two containers standing next to each other. One side of this house still had all four sides of the container intact for privacy reasons, but the other side featured a sliding door with a fold-out deck.

I walked through this little house for only a minute or two, but I thought about it for days after. Three things stood out to me. First was the size of the thing. Yes, it was small compared to my current four-bedroom home, but it was actually much larger than the closet disguised as a flat that I started out in.

Secondly, it was aesthetically pleasing—not so much the rectangular shape, but rather the modular design. I liked the idea that you could seemingly keep adding to it by simply buying another container. It was like Lego, but for grown-ups.

Finally, I loved the idea that it seemed mobile. Not mobile like a recreational vehicle, but easier to transport than the things normally used to build a house. Containers are, after all, a standardized size. That doesn't make things easier just for shipping over water, but also for fitting on trucks as well.

Reasons to Go Tiny

There is a cost factor involved, but in this chapter, the cost will only be discussed broadly. As you can imagine, there are a few other things to consider, like the law. I'll get into that thoroughly in the next chapter, giving you a proper breakdown of how to set up your own shipping container house. For now, I'm simply going to focus on the costs of getting a shipping container home.

Cost

There are three ways you can go about getting your hands on a shipping container house, but before we get to that, we first need to look at the sizes. Shipping containers are meant to be modular, which means they have a standard slotting mechanism and width, but you can get them in various lengths. In more recent times, you can also get containers that are slightly taller than what most of us consider standard. And by "standard" I mean the shipping containers you've seen scattered across the country, but never really thought about.

Containers are most common in 20ft and 40ft lengths, though you can find other sizes, and all can be used to build a home. The most commonly used as a basis is a 40ft general container. Having said that, there are many ways to go about it. I've seen homes based around three 20ft containers, or one 40ft and one 20ft.

The main thing to remember here is the various lengths, as well as the kind of container you're after. A standard container is a closed unit with one opening door, but you can find containers that open on both ends, as well as units with fold-out doors on the sides.

The average price, at the time of writing, is $2400 to $2750 for a 10ft, $1800 to $3060 for a 20ft, and $1850 to $5300 for a 40ft.

The price differences you see above are between new and used. A new container will likely be sold with a 5-year guarantee, while a used container would have already served some time at sea. Don't be afraid to buy used, however. Used containers come with grading, and the most commonly-used term is WWT. This stands for wind & watertight, which is exactly what you need it to be. This grading is according to Container Services International's *Used Container Certification and Grading* (2020).

What this means is that you can buy a bare-bones 40ft container for as little as $1850, and you have the basis of a shipping container house.

According to Perino and Davis's article *Here's the Typical Home Price in Every State — and What You Can Actually Get for That Money* (2020), the average median price for a home in the USA is $247,084. A brand-new 40ft container costs a fraction of that. Sure, some costs will be added along the way to bring it closer to the average cost of a house, but it's nice knowing that you can have a roof and four walls for as little as $1800.

With that being said, if you are going to be tackling this project by yourself to keep costs as low as possible, you need to be able to do a little bit of everything. In other words, you'll need to be a handyman of sorts. At the moment we're just talking about an empty container, but before you live in it, that container will require some sort of insulation, an electrical supply, plumbing, and gas.

Once you factor all of that in, the cost will quickly escalate beyond $10,000. That's if you buy all the materials you need and do all of the installation work yourself.

If you're not that savvy with a saw, fear not. There are multiple pre-made options available, and there have been for some time. In fact, Amazon actually made the news back in 2017 for being the first online delivery service to sell an actual house.

The house in question cost $36,000, not including the $4,500 shipping fee. For that, you received a converted brand-new 40ft container. The price included a bedroom, kitchen, shower, toilet, furniture, and all appliances. More importantly, it easily plugged into existing sewer, electrical, and water supply systems.

Having said that, it's certainly not the most attractive proposition out there. The design was function over form, so it looked more like a bunker than anything else—nowhere near what you and I would refer to as luxurious. Still, if all you require is a roof over your head, a kitchen to cook in, and a place to sleep, it checks all those basic boxes.

Luckily, a few years have passed since the introduction of that specific container house, and since then a few companies have jumped up to fill the need for a more stylish container house. Companies like Alternative Living Spaces, Honomobo, Kubed Living, Custom Container Living, and Backcountry Containers all offer completely built container homes. In most cases, you can even customize the home to suit your own needs and taste.

There's a lot of variety out there, and a home to suit every budget. There are 160 square foot, two-sleeper cabins that retail for $32,999, attractive 40ft, two-bedroom homes in the $50,000 bracket, and high-end luxury 40ft homes that retail around the $100,000 mark. One can even go larger than that and build a full-size home out of containers. There are pre-built options for around $220,000 that come with large living areas, a garage, and a fireplace.

These high-end container houses may seem irrelevant since they cost as much as an actual house, but think about it from a different perspective. In the most expensive states, it's almost always a land issue. There's very limited availability and therefore it's extremely expensive. Far more expensive than it is to actually build a house. When you combine the two, you end up with a colossal figure.

With that in mind, consider that you can buy a piece of prime land and get around the additional cost of building a property on it by investing in a large container home. It won't be a movable structure, but you'll have a house in an affluent area for much less than it would have cost to buy the land, hire an architect to design a house, and finally get contractors in to build it.

There's also a solution between buying a basic, empty shipping container and buying a ready-built shipping container home.

Because this is an emerging trend, and one that's getting some serious attention at the moment, companies have started offering standard containers with windows, doors, and sliding glass doors installed. There are various companies that offer these options, with a used 40ft container costing roughly $15,000.

You'll have a bare shell, but let's say you had a budget of $100,000 in mind, or roughly half of what an actual house costs on average. That leaves you with $85,000 to spend on interior design, and everything else we'll cover in chapter two. HomeGuide's *2020*

Cost To Build a House (2020) offers an extensive breakdown of how much it costs to build any house, including shipping container homes.

The costs vary significantly depending on where you are, but the worst-case scenario you're looking at is $40,000 to fit a container with insulation, drywall, all the necessary interior and exterior fittings, and furniture.

It's difficult to work on averages when it comes to contractor rates. In the cheaper states, you're looking at around $80 per square foot, while the most expensive states cost double that.

As you can see, there are many different options available. If we take the median price for a home in the USA and cut it in half, we get $123,500. Take away another $20,000 for all the legalities (more on than later), and you still end up with $100,000 left for a shipping container house.

For half the price of the average American home, you can build something pretty spectacular.

Environmental Impact

If you buy a used container, you're already one step ahead when it comes to lessening the overall environmental impact of homeownership. It's basically taking one thing that's no longer suited to its main purpose and using it for something else, otherwise known as recycling. To most, recycling is already enough of a selling point, but it goes much further than that.

The amount of concrete needed for a container house is insignificant compared to a normal house. You only need a foundation, which will be much smaller than the foundation of a normal house. Considering how destructive the manufacturing of concrete is to the environment, this is another step in the right direction.

Then we get to the size of the house. A smaller house requires less energy to heat and cool, and you have a flat surface on top of which you can mount solar panels for that purpose.

Durability

The average American home is built out of a collection of wood, iron, cement, and concrete. It's a strong, robust recipe that has served the nation well, which is why you might hesitate to move over to a steel box.

Take a minute to consider what that box's intended purpose was. It was designed to retain its original shape while being transported thousands of miles around the world. And it had to do so with other containers stacked around it, facing the harshest weather conditions you can imagine. We're talking 100-mile an hour winds and a constant lashing of seawater, which is highly corrosive. They spend an average of 10 to 12 years at sea before they're retired, but even then, most of them retain their WWT rating.

If it can withstand all of that, it will likely survive a moderate climate, the average storm, and even a hurricane. You just need to bolster it with a proper foundation, and it will hold on for dear life.

While we're on the topic of Mother Nature, it's worth noting that storms aren't the only thing she might send your way. Depending on where you live, you might also have to deal with ants, termites, spiders, raccoons, and bears.

The insects will have no interest in your steel box, while the bigger critters will have a harder time breaking into it. When it comes down to it, would you rather have a thick piece of steel or a piece of wood standing between you and a curious bear?

Now that we've looked at the positives of shipping container homes, it's only fair we discuss the downsides as well.

The main problem with steel is that it rusts. But considering that these things were designed to face the high seas, the designers have made them as rust-proof as possible. The first layer is rust-proof paint, but over time it wears down or is scratched during use. Behind that layer, you'll find weathering steel, specifically designed to rust in layers to prevent deep rusting problems.

When buying a container, this is something to look out for. A shallow layer of rust on the outside is nothing to be concerned about. It can be sanded down to the steel surface and recoated with rust-proof paint. Once it's on dry land, it won't be bashing against other things as much, so the paint should last longer. Having said that, it's worth inspecting at least once a year, if not once a month.

Another thing to keep in mind if you're tackling this project by yourself is structural rigidity. You can remove certain sections of a container to install windows and sliding doors, but remove too much, and the whole thing could collapse in on itself. You should be particularly careful when stacking two or more for a bigger house. It's definitely worth paying for a structural engineer to come have a look and give some advice as to where you can insert extra structural strength.

Flexibility

As I stated earlier, container houses are a bit like Lego for grown-ups. Or perhaps giant-sized Lego you can live in is a more apt description.

If we look at the International Organization of Standardization's (ISO) guide for shipping container strength, we see that they're designed strong enough to carry eight other fully-loaded containers on top. That's likely much higher than you'll ever need to go.

The modular layout also means that you can let your imagination run wild when it comes to designing a house. You could stack two 40ft containers on top of each other and have a double-story house with the living area downstairs and a large bedroom upstairs. Or you could have a 40ft container as the main living area, a 20ft as a bedroom, and a small 10ft as an entrance.

In larger constructions, the sides can be removed completely, and the containers welded securely side-by-side. This makes it possible to have a more spacious floor plan.

Easy to move

My initial assessment that you can simply buy a piece of land and place a container home wherever you want was right. You can do it in certain places, but you most definitely don't want to.

Even a container house requires a foundation, which we shall delve into deeper in the next chapter.

For now, you just need to know that you can make a container house easier to move depending on which foundation you go for. The choice of foundation is not up to you, however. Areas with regular rainfall obviously require a more solid foundation, while dry, semi-desert areas often require nothing more than a basic wooden or concrete structure.

As it turns out, shipping container homes aren't as easy to move around as you might have originally thought, but it's not impossible. There's just a heap of red tape standing between you and moving said container home between two locations, but if you're willing to go through it, more power to you.

Design Ideas

Interior

There's something rugged and industrial about the interior of a container. I find it pleasing to the eye, especially in a darker shade of blue, combined with wooden furniture. Some choose to leave the interior walls of their container house as is, but for some, this is simply not a possibility.

The main consideration is the weather. In places where you'll have to stave off either extreme hot or cold, insulation is needed. Most people opt for sheetrock or paneling on top of this insulation. Both are attractive and can be done to suit your own personal taste. The same is true of the roof. It can be kept as is, but it's worth placing an extra layer in there if only to provide a gap where electrical wiring can run, and something fixtures can be mounted to.

The good news is that the floor of a standard container should already be equipped with a subfloor, in most cases made of plywood. It's a hard-wearing surface, meant for years of abuse, so it should still hold up to any sort of modification. You can cover it with tiles, carpet, concrete, or vinyl.

Exterior

Some people opt to let some of the origins of the house shine through, while there are those who prefer to get as far away from the origins as possible. The best example of this is a triangular design, made up of three containers—two underneath and one stacked on top. The entire structure is then covered in wood paneling, including the triangular section between the top of the stacked containers and the top of the container standing on the side. Standing next to a structure like this, you'd be hard-pressed to tell the difference between it and a normal house.

As the exterior decoration mostly serves a style function, there are as many designs as there are people. I've seen container houses decorated to look like country cottages in England, a few that are modern enough to feature in an art exhibition, and quite a few that retain their shabby exterior, only to dazzle you once you're inside.

When it comes to the exterior, the main thing you want to consider is the layout. As I've said before, the modular layout allows for an almost limitless amount of designs, but the more creative you get, the more careful you have to be with regards to structural rigidity. Especially once you start stacking.

I find the stacking fascinating. It's something humans figured out decades ago. If you don't have enough space to go horizontally, you move upward. Imagine the square footage you can get by stacking, with a main floor made of two containers with the center parts removed. It will be a massive living area, while the main bedroom will be the third container stacked on top.

If space is a concern, consider a "U" shape. I've seen it used many times before, as you get the maximum amount of floor space by using three containers—two 40ft and one 20ft. The two 40ft containers are stacked parallel, while the 20ft forms the bottom of the "U."

When used correctly, this method results in a massive living space between the two large containers. It obviously requires a bigger foundation, and the additional cost of building a roof over the "U," shape, but it's still nowhere near what a traditional house costs to build.

The two larger containers can be used as luxurious bedrooms with en-suite bathrooms, while the space in the middle is used as a living area. The 20ft container can be used as a purpose-built kitchen.

The possibilities are endless, but the main thing to keep in mind is that you don't want to start stacking without professional input. We know the ISO standard states that one standard container should be able to hold eight fully-loaded containers on top, but the ISO standard is for a container with no modifications.

When it comes to housing, the bottom container will always be structurally compromised, because the owner obviously needs a door and windows.

Many Other Applications

While researching this book, I came across containers used in many other applications that are going to be particularly relevant in the post-pandemic world.

There are many unique uses for shipping container structures. I've even seen a ski resort built entirely out of containers. Not only do they contrast beautifully with the surroundings, but they make business sense as well. Many ski resorts around the globe are only operational for a small portion of the year. They rely entirely on the income from a three-month period to cover costs for an entire year, so it makes perfect sense to build a hotel that costs a fraction of what a traditional brick and mortar hotel would have been. The cost of heating these units are also much less, once again bringing operational costs down and increasing profits.

If you're lucky enough to be fully employed still and working remotely, there's a good chance that will become the norm going forward. Now that the idea of remote working has become the norm, it makes sense that businesses will be removing the overhead cost of renting a building to house staff.

This may be perfect for them, but your situation at home may not be ideal. I'm lucky enough to have my own office at home. If the kids get too noisy, I can close the door. The last place I want to work at is the kitchen table, with people constantly in and out, not to mention the many distractions I can see from there.

I think a 10ft container would make a lovely office away from home, even if it's just in the garden.

We can't move over to the next chapter before considering the charitable applications of container houses. The best example I could find was in South Africa, which is using shipping containers to great effect.

The law in South Africa doesn't force companies to partake in Corporate Social Responsibility (CSR), but they are awarded a public interest score at the end of every financial year (Kirby, 2018). These points, amongst many other factors, count whenever a government contract is awarded. Beyond this, many of the companies that operate in South Africa are international conglomerates, including mining and manufacturing. These billion-dollar companies are expected to contribute to or engage with at least one (or in most cases, many) charitable organizations. The companies are happy to do so because it reflects positively in terms of public relations, and it helps them build a positive image within the country.

Having said that, many companies do not operate in the billion-dollar league and don't have entire departments dedicated to public relations. All they have to offer is money, which isn't a bad thing. It's just how it is.

These companies will often approach a third party and pay them to do CSR on their behalf, and that's where a company like Big Box comes in.

The basic premise is that a company approaches Big Box, tells them what charitable organization they want to contribute to, and they see what they can come up with.

Big Box specializes in converting containers specifically for those who need it most. They can convert a container into almost anything at a cost-effective price.

One example is the Mandela Day Library Project. South Africans celebrate Mandela Day on July 18 every year and dedicate 67 minutes of their time to something charitable. The 67 minutes comes from the 67 years Nelson Mandela spent fighting for social justice.

Big companies celebrate the day properly and come to the table with giant contributions. Container libraries are just one of these many contributions. To date, Big Box has opened seventy-five 40ft libraries, granting access to books in the county's rural areas. Over 71,000 people now have access to books for the first time.

Big Box can also build computer labs, smart classrooms, bathrooms, and even skate parks. All of this is done at a fraction of the cost, and in remote locations where building would be nearly impossible.

It's not just the third world using shipping containers for charitable needs. In the United Kingdom, they are now being used to house the homeless, though not without controversy.

As reported by Patrick Butler (2019), a block of container flats large enough to house 60 families, went up in just 24 weeks. That may seem like a long time, but it's quite fast considering how long it usually takes to build in historic London.

Unfortunately, the UK suffered a heatwave that summer, recording temperatures of 34 degrees Celsius. This had a drastic effect on the top floor of the four-story building, making the interior of the shipping container homes too hot to live in. There was also a problem with condensation.

This is a common mistake and one that I referred to earlier. A container house should be fine in moderate to mild climates, but in severe temperatures, insulation and cooling are needed.

As noted in the article, a member of the public who lives there noted these issues, as well as the space constraints, but also noted that the alternative would have been much worse.

I regard it as a lesson learned. This took place in 2019, which means first-world governments are now noticing how quickly and cheaply container homes can be erected for those who need them most. Because it's still early days, there are some issues that need to be ironed out, but I can definitely see a case for container homes being used to house the homeless.

Perhaps more aptly, I can see them being used as temporary housing for displaced individuals. We live in a country where thousands are evacuated every year due to the weather or fires. Basic container homes can be transported from a central facility to anywhere in the USA in one or two days, providing cover in emergency situations. These examples are just a few of the many possible ways that shipping container homes might be used in the years to come.

Chapter 2: The Building Process

For many people, one of the most attractive elements of a shipping container home is the idea that you can simply pick it up, slap it on the back of a truck, and drive it to somewhere new whenever you feel like it.

Turns out it's not as simple as that, but for very good reason. As you'll see in this chapter, most of the rules and regulations are aimed at safety.

But before we get to that, allow me to talk you through the whole process of building a shipping container home, from where you purchase it, to the moment you move in.

Find Inspiration

Once you have an idea of what you might want your home to look like, you can set up a shopping list of needs. You need to know the basic layout, so you know what size container you need to purchase. As a reminder, they're usually available in 10ft, 20ft, and 40ft. The latter is also available as a high-cube, which is one foot taller than a standard container.

You also need to keep an eye out for specially-built containers. A sealed, heavily-modified or refrigerated container is of no use when it comes to building a container house.

At this point in time, you should already have a site in mind. You could either purchase a piece of land or rent it.

While an off-the-grid site, far from any breathing soul, might seem romantic, you need to think logically about where you want to live. If you go too far off the grid, it will be difficult and expensive to get connected to utilities. Going to the store will also be a hardship, not to mention the fact that you'll be far away from medical care and the police. Unless you're serious about living off the grid completely, find a spot that's within appropriate distance of a town that has all the basics you'll need.

Where to Buy a Shipping Container

Thanks to the rise in popularity of new and used shipping containers, finding one to buy is as easy as typing "buy a shipping container" in the Google search engine. You'll note that most containers are for sale in harbor towns and cities.

There are large companies that specialize in selling used containers, but it's worth pointing out that you can get a shipping container for much cheaper on Craigslist and eBay. And as I said in the first chapter, you can also buy a ready-made container home on Amazon. You can also bid on a container on Shipped.com. They offer delivery included in the price.

By now you're already familiar with the various sizes on offer, but it's worth looking at the grading system again.

We'll start with new. To get to wherever you are, it already had to be shipped at least once, but that's nothing to be concerned about. The pros are that it's the most robust container you can possibly buy, and will most likely come with a guarantee of some sort. The con to this type of container is obviously the price.

The second condition is cargo-worthy. These containers still have their sea legs and a few trips left in them. The guarantee is less likely, but the condition will still be good. It will cost less than a new container, but still a fair amount more than a fully-fledged used container.

Next up is used with a WWT rating. This is a used container that has served its purpose but is still windproof and weatherproof.

Last, we have used containers that are sold as-is. These are not worth the time, as they most likely have dents, holes, or irreparable rust problems.

If you can buy new, it's worth the added peace of mind, but a used container still has a lot of life left in it. The main thing to keep an eye on is the WWT rating.

Shipping a Shipping Container

To some, the cost of transporting a container across the land will be a deal-breaker.

The cost depends on two things: The size of the container, and the price of diesel. The smaller the shipping container, the cheaper it will be to transport. Unfortunately, the most commonly used size is 40ft, which happens to be the most expensive, as it requires a large truck with some sort of tilt trailer or integrated crane.

Fortunately, this is something you can also shop around for online. It's not a service dominated by one single business, which also leaves room for negotiation. Given the current economic climate, one might even say that prices are highly negotiable.

Having said that, there are a few things to consider. Shipping within a 100-mile radius costs more per mile than shipping within a 300-mile radius. The price comes down as the mileage goes up, but it never gets to a point where you'd call it cheap.

To find out what it would cost to ship a container, I approached a few companies for a quote. The quotes varied wildly, so I decided to rather work on a worst-case scenario average. In this case, it's $5 per mile. I prefer to work with the worst-case scenario and have you feel like you saved some money, rather than work everything out at the cheapest price possible, which can't then be replicated.

With that figure in mind, it's easy to see why any aspirations of a shipping container house might go right out the window once you factor in the cost of transport.

Let's say there's a 40ft container for sale in Los Angeles at a reasonable price. The end destination is Oak City, Utah. The fastest route is via Highway 91, and the total mileage is 573 miles. Worst-case scenario, the cost of transporting one 40ft trailer works out to $2,875. If you purchased a used container, the price of having it delivered is actually more than the container itself. The further north you move, the more expensive it gets. You could always go along the shoreline and find the closest port, but this limits the available shipping containers.

Even when you factor in the high price of transport, a container home still works out cheaper than a normal house. But if you set yourself a budget of $100,000 for example, it's worth keeping all these additional costs in mind so that you don't reach your budget too quickly.

Prepare the Site

Before the container arrives at the site, there's a lot of prep work to do. The area where the container will be standing needs to be cleared properly, and you need temporary mountings to keep the container on until the build is finished. You can use wood, tires, or even temporary steel structures specifically designed for this purpose.

That's if you're planning on first getting all the necessary building material there before the build starts, which I recommend.

I think it's worth investing in a few experts during the process. The most important expert you want to involve is a contractor experienced with shipping container house foundations.

A shipping container by itself is extremely strong, but you have no control over what's going on underneath it. When simply put down on the ground, a shipping container is at the mercy of ground movements. Take heavy rain as an example. We've all seen how quickly heavy rain can erode ground and cause mudslides. Now imagine the rain eroding the ground around and underneath the container.

Other things you might consider are the view, how easy the shipping container house can be accessed, proximity to the electricity supply, and how close the gas lines and sewage pipes are. You might also want to study the geological history of the site to see if it's prone to any kind of problem, like erosion.

Foundations

There are four kinds of foundations available for container homes, and you'd use them for different applications.

The first and most used example is the pier foundation. It's basically a concrete and iron block at each corner of the container, with another set in the middle for a 40ft container. This foundation doesn't require a lot of digging. Each leg is 20 inches wide and deep, and the container mounts neatly on top. You don't require professional help for this particular foundation, as it's quite easy to set up.

In some states, the ground is too soft for a pile foundation, which means you have to go deeper to find stable ground. This requires a lot of digging at first, after which solid steel tubes are inserted deep enough to find stable ground. These steel pipes (piles) are further strengthened with concrete.

Once a pile foundation is secure, it doesn't look all that different from a pier foundation, but it's not a project you can tackle by yourself. Knowing when the ground is stable enough and mixing the right kind of concrete is a job best left to the experts, especially when you're dealing with soft ground. This is the most expensive foundation available, but also the most secure.

A slab foundation is exactly what it sounds like. You dig deep, lay a big slab of concrete that's a few inches wider than the house, and you're ready to go. It does have a few drawbacks, however. Due to the amount of concrete used, it is a more expensive option. It's also not suitable for states where severe cold weather is a problem. The heat in the container house eventually siphons down into the ground once the foundation gets colder than the interior of the house.

Finally, slab foundations are a pain if you have problems with pipes. With a pier or a pile foundation, you can simply dig down to where the problem is and fix it. With a slab, the pipe is entirely covered under a few feet of concrete.

Finally, there's a combination of foundations called the strip foundation. It's like a slab, but only in strips. It doesn't cover the whole area, but only certain parts. This is a good way to save money, but be aware that a strip foundation doesn't hold up well against earthquakes.

In each of these foundations, a steel pipe is inserted into the concrete while it is curing. This will later be used to mount the container to the foundation. If, however, you find a suitable foundation without mounts, you can use a concrete anchor.

When it comes to concrete, I always recommend hiring an expert.

People spend decades learning to work with concrete. It's such a sensitive material that its strength can be compromised when you don't mix it correctly on a cold day. I'd go as far as calling it a science, which means you need a specialist.

Utilities

When they're browsing Instagram, looking at all those wonderful shipping container houses and wondering whether it will work for them, this is the part most people forget about. Somehow, you'll need electricity, gas, water, and a way to get rid of sewage.

The first and most obvious utility you'll need is electricity. Why? Well, you're going to need it to build the home. Building with shipping containers requires electricity for welding, mixing concrete, and of course, making coffee. It's like any other building site, and it's going to be expensive to run a site on just a generator.

Electrical services depend on state and service providers. Some service providers will happily connect you to the grid, even if it costs them a few poles and a transformer. The idea is that they'll make a profit off you in the long run, especially if others will eventually join you in the area. Other service providers stipulate a certain length of cable they're willing to lay down before you have to cover the cost yourself. Then there are companies that might not even be interested if they can't see the merit in the project. It's worth shopping around to find the deal that works for you.

At least gas is easy to sort out. Big cities have natural gas lines that you simply plug into, but out in rural areas, one has to rely on tanks. It's not all that difficult to install. You just need to ensure there are no leaks, but that's easy enough to do using water. The only hindrance when it comes to gas is that you'll need to have the gas tank filled every once in a while. Depending on how large it is, this could be a once a month exercise.

Like electricity, getting connected to sewage lines depends entirely on how far off the grid you want to be. If there is easy access to a line, it's worth going for it; otherwise, an underground tank is the only option. The upfront cost of these tanks can be as high as $5,000, not including the digging of a hole and the installation. On the upside, they require little upkeep after the fact.

Water delivery isn't a problem in the USA. Even the most remote locations can be connected, and you really have to be properly off the grid to have water problems. Even so, you might want to look at a storage tank. You can get clean water trucked in once a month. You can also investigate a well, if the area you're looking at is suitable for it. As I said earlier, if you want to be as environmentally friendly as possible, it's worth investing in a tank to harvest rainwater.

Get Specialists for Specialist Jobs

Welding always looks so easy on TV, right? Turns out it's not, no matter how many YouTube tutorials you watch. Unless you really are familiar with welding and structural rigidity, I urge you to hire a specialist for a few days.

The problem is that we know shipping containers can handle the loads, but there simply isn't an existing standard for these things once you start cutting out windows, and doors. Every piece of steel you remove compromises the strength of the container underneath. And it's not just that. Once you start welding, you want to do a good enough job to keep the rust out.

At some point, your container house will have to be inspected before it can be deemed safe to live in. That means you should get an architect or engineer involved in the planning phase to give some much-needed advice. The last thing you want is to fail the final inspection.

While all of this may take time in the beginning, it will save you time in the end. And you have to ask yourself, is it worth taking risks when it comes to structural rigidity?

Set Up a Schedule

Before you tackle this project head-on, it's worth investigating and planning it properly.

Not only is it good to know exactly what you're in for, but it's good to know how long the process will take.

The biggest time suck will be planning and selecting materials. Following that, it will be the transportation of the containers and the foundation. After that, you can look at another two weeks to fit insulation, drywall, and fittings. And then, following an inspection, can you move your furniture in.

It's worth setting up this schedule to know what kind of ride you can expect. Yes, container houses can be built quickly, but only relative to the time it takes to build a normal house.

A good estimate is around 18 weeks from start to finish, and that's if everything runs smoothly, and all the contractors' work is done on time.

Zoning and Permits

The legal jargon surrounding shipping container homes is a minefield, mostly because it's regulated at a state level. Some states are fairly open to the idea, whereas the governing bodies of other states are less inclined to give you permission.

It's impossible to include the regulations for every state in this book, but I can give you advice on the various regulations you might face and how to navigate them.

Before you tackle this section, it's worth getting your ducks in a row. In addition to having your plans in full, you need to be able to describe exactly what your container house will be. This is due to the fact that the definition of "container house" is open to interpretation. You need to be able to tell whomever exactly how big your house will be, what it will be used for, and how many people will be living there.

With that in mind, let's look at all the red tape standing between you and your dream shipping container house.

Zoning

Zoning is used by cities and counties to break up the land for various purposes. In other words, they decide where the people live, where they shop, where manufacturing takes place, where crops are grown, and where schools are built.

It seems like a hassle, but the regulations are there to keep people safe. A school would never be built in an industrial area, for example. The same regulations keep noisy clubs out of residential areas.

There are many different zone designations, but the main designations that concern you as the future owner of a container house are residential. Once you know what zones were set aside for residential areas, you can study the zone designations more carefully to decide where you want to live.

It's much easier following the existing zoning codes than it is to change them. The law allows for rezoning, but this will cost you a hefty amount in court fees, not to mention a few other people that will also have to buy into the concept. The chances of the courts changing zoning regulations for one individual are slim to none.

Codes and Permits

These codes are designed to keep you safe, as there are certain standards a building needs to adhere to before it can be occupied. This is the number one reason why you should get an expert opinion before starting a build.

The good news is that US building codes are based on codes developed by the International Code Council. These codes were developed specifically for developed countries and they include everything from plumbing, electric, fire standards—really everything involved in building a home.

For the most part, it's a standard set of rules you can download from your state's official website, but it's worth keeping in mind that there are certain states with specific rules. It may take a while, but it's worth getting your hands on this document and working it through thoroughly. Ignoring the rules can result in far more than just a fine. In certain states, you will be ordered to tear the construction down and start over.

The only problem with international codes is that they're written in the kind of language the average person will struggle to understand. If at any point you feel overwhelmed by the document, make a notation and remember to ask about it when you go see a professional.

Classification

The classification of a container home matters, because it decides whether the standards you'll have to adhere to fall under federal building codes or local building codes. Homes that are built in a factory and shipped out to be erected on an existing platform fall under federal regulations.

The reason this area is so difficult to define is the existence of recreational vehicles. There are certain container houses that can be mounted directly to a truck chassis, which means they fall into the same category as recreational vehicles. These vehicles have their own set of standards, as you can imagine.

So, which set of standards to use? There has been some confusion over the years, but since the rise in popularity, some clarity has emerged.

Since most shipping container homes will be mounted on an existing foundation, the same rules apply to them as any other house. This may seem unfair, but I think it helps. There's no murky water to wade through. Your container house has to be built to the same standards as a normal house, which are clearly defined in the international building codes.

Deeds and Restrictions

The government might not be the only thing standing in your way. The deed of your property or the rules of the homeowners association might keep you from building your dream shipping container home.

A deed is more difficult to change than a homeowner's association guide. The former usually requires a court order, while the latter requires a vote of the involved homeowners.

A homeowner's association can be a tricky entity to work with since they're mostly responsible for maintaining order when it comes to what your house and your garden can look like.

This association will typically regulate the color of your house, the style of the roof, landscaping, and distance from the neighbors.

It can be tricky to build a container house that follows the exact design guidelines, given how it's basically only available as a rectangle, but there are means.

Who is in charge of ensuring compliance?

The good news is that most building codes and zoning are done on a municipal level, which means you won't have to go knock on the White House's door if you want to paint your house a new color.

As I said earlier, it's best to familiarize yourself with the building codes and zoning regulations before you start building. In this case, it's most certainly better to make sure you have permission, rather than to ask for forgiveness.

The step up from that is county regulation. This has more weight in rural areas, where regulations aren't as strict.

A step up from that is the state, which only enforces state-specific requirements. If you live in a hurricane zone, your plans will have to include the state-mandated requirements. A similar stipulation is true for earthquake-prone California.

On a federal level, there's only one code, and it's the previously mentioned law for manufactured homes on a chassis. Since RVs can travel across state lines, it makes sense that they're the only dwelling regulated on a federal level.

The key takeaway from this chapter is to do things the right way. Looking at amazing images of shipping container houses, you might be tempted to immediately purchase two 40ft containers and get going.

The smart way to do it is to first see what's allowed at a municipal level, whether the land you're interested in may be used for that purpose, and whether you can get everything you need within the budget you set. Only when you can answer yes to all those questions, should you proceed.

The Best States for Container Homes

While there are a lot of hoops to jump through, there are some states that caught on early and have made it easier to set up a shipping container house. In most states, residential areas are open to the idea, though you should prepare yourself to do a lot of explaining.

But not if you live in Texas, Tennessee, Louisiana, Missouri, Oregon, or Alaska. Texas already has thousands of container homes, some of which are even up for sale. You might expect California to be a nightmare when it comes to container houses, but given that it's a modern state that prides itself on being at the forefront of technology, it has been more accepting than most.

As for the rest of the states mentioned above, they all have lenient, easy to change zoning laws. It also helps that they have wide open, rural space available, which makes it easier to be lenient when it comes to the business of erecting a house.

What Does the Future Hold?

There is a remarkable difference between the opinions of shipping container houses in 2015 and now.

Most of the opinion articles I've read, dating back as far as 2012, were of the opinion that shipping container houses were nothing more than a trend for the rich. The general consensus was that it was a fabulous way for the rich to build a second or even third house without spending too much.

Due to the pandemic, there has been renewed interest in shipping container houses, naturally followed by new opinion pieces. There are many that are still extremely skeptical about the idea, mostly because they believe that most people won't be willing to sacrifice space in order to save money. There's also an argument that container houses aren't as cheap as one might think, and I made a point of demonstrating that in this book. Yes, it's not as easy as simply buying a container and living in it, but compared to the average price of a normal house in the USA, there's no denying that shipping container houses are much cheaper. Even if you have the thing built for you, it's still cheaper.

Shipping container homes are no longer just a trend, but a realistic alternative that can ensure that you still have enough money left over to buy the basic necessities.

Even before the pandemic, futurists were making predictions that humans would move away from the traditional housing system. Faith Popcorn, renowned futurist and author, compiled an interesting look at what the future holds when it comes to housing. The piece is titled *A New Kind of Cocoon: The House of Tomorrow* (2020).

In this piece, Popcorn mentions nomadism and the sharing economy. It basically boils down to Millennials not being able to afford traditional housing, leading to them shunning spacious apartments in favor of tiny living. The most important statistic mentioned in this piece is the year-on-year increase in the sale of tiny houses. Compared to 2018, 2019 saw an increase of 67%. That's not just an incremental growth, but rather a large leap towards a realistic alternative.

And it's not just out of necessity either. Millennials and Generation Z are big on self-expression. They want their dwelling to be a reflection of who they are as a person, and there simply isn't another building method that offers you so much variety in terms of what you can do with shipping container architecture.

Finally, it's a well-known fact that younger generations are more concerned about the environment than the rest of us ever were. Shipping containers aren't simply environmentally friendly to begin with, but they can be adapted more easily to exist entirely off the grid and require far less material to modify.

Many people are still of the opinion that this is a passing fad. They mention that shipping containers aren't as environmentally friendly as we'd like to believe, especially when you buy them new.

There are also problems with temperature regulation, as well as housing codes and zoning.

The temperature regulation problem, in my humble opinion, is a teething issue. It can easily be fixed by installing some sort of temperature regulating system. The housing and zoning codes are not as easy to fix, as you need numbers to change those. But when you look at the 67% increase in tiny home purchases, you can't help but wonder whether a change is on the horizon.

This so-called trend is set to grow to a size where local and state governments can't ignore it.

Chapter 3: What's Tiny Home Living Like?

While you can build a large shipping container home, many people choose to build a scaled-down, minimalistic home instead. I spent some time living in a small shipping container home, and the first thing that struck me about living in a tiny home is how it forces you to be neater. As an avid reader, I'm constantly busy reading at least four books at any one time. It's not a problem at my current house, which has two living rooms and twice as many bedrooms. I can leave my books lying all over the place, and the house still looks neat.

The same can't be said for the tiny container house. You leave just one book on the table and the entire thing looks untidy. The same is true if you don't wash the dishes, or leave clothes on the floor, or anything along those lines.

A tiny house means every single thing has its space, and if it's not in that space, the place is untidy. I hate being untidy, so I found myself constantly tidying up the place. At least it was small, so it was only a five-minute job.

If I had to design my own container house, I'd definitely want a door between my sleeping quarters and the rest of the house.

The second thing that stood out is the way it changes where you do things. I found that we were only in the house when it was absolutely necessary, to complete some sort of function, like sleeping, cooking, or going to the bathroom.

We spent the rest of our time outdoors in the garden or on the veranda, doing things we'd normally do indoors. We'd have dinner outside, entertain guests outside, and even read outside. The small scale really forces you to make use of your garden, which we tend to take for granted.

The third thing I loved was the efficiency. The weather was mild, so we had hot days and cool nights. Not only did the container heat and cool quickly, but it was done efficiently as well. This was all done with power harvested by the sun thanks to a neat array of solar panels. The power is stored in a power bank, which was neatly integrated on the outside. I must admit that the idea of having such a powerful battery mounted on a steel box had me worried for a bit, but I was assured that it was installed by a professional and that we had nothing to worry about. Once I got over that fear, it was nice knowing that we were contributing a grand total of zero grams of CO_2 to the environment.

After a few days, a shopping trip was necessary, and we soon found another upside of tiny living. It's not conducive to shopping for self-gratification, which is basically programmed into human nature. I think container living would be a joy for anyone living a minimalist lifestyle. There are only so many things you can have, which may be annoying to some. Personally, I found it deeply refreshing.

Finally, there was the cost of the thing. The container house we were living in cost roughly $80,000, and I kept on thinking what the equivalent normal house would look like. For the record, I couldn't find anything in that price bracket, which goes a long way toward explaining why younger people are much quicker to adopt this trend.

It's basically a choice between renting and paying for someone else's house, or buying/building your own home for a third of the price. Not a tough choice to make, I'm sure you'll agree.

I have to admit that there are some downsides to tiny living as well.

The first negative is also a positive. A tiny house forces you to spend more time outside, which is nice when the weather is mild, but not so nice when it's extremely hot or cold. I can only imagine what it must feel like for a whole family to be stuck in a 40ft container because it's too cold to go outside.

Which brings me to my second issue. It was lovely sharing my space with the wife and kids for the first few days, but after that, I was longing for a space of my own. No amount of walking can replace a room of your very own like I have at home. My wife admitted to feeling the same way, but perhaps that's just something you eventually make peace with.

Finally, there was nowhere for my stuff. I'm an impulsive book buyer, and I had to give up numerous purchases because there wasn't enough room in the tiny house. I can hardly blame the house, however. It was not designed with my specific needs in mind, which brings us neatly to the next topic of discussion.

Buy or Build?

There are many companies that can pre-build you a container house. It's a simple, elegant solution to the housing crisis that serves a very specific portion of the population. Rather than spending an exorbitant amount of money on a normal house you most likely can't afford, why not buy a smaller starter home and work your way from there.

I can definitely see the argument for pre-built container houses. Mass production brings costs down compared to individually designed units.

It depends entirely on where you are in your life. Simply want a safe place to sleep in at a fraction of the cost you're used to? Then buy a pre-made tiny container house and enjoy it.

But if you have a specific set of requirements, it's worth doing all the research, finding the right containers, and hiring the right contractors to build the space exactly as you want it.

I think a tiny container house is another way to express your personality. I'd want my tiny house to reflect a bit of my own personality to the outside world.

Financing

As cheap as some of these options may be, few people have $100 lying around, let alone $100,000.

The good news is that there are financing options available. You could go the old-school mortgage route, or, apply for a personal loan. As long as your shipping container house is built within the guidelines of whatever municipality you want to build in, you can apply for a loan.

Real estate has always been a popular investment because it rarely loses value. At this point in time, it's hard to tell whether the same is true when it comes to container houses.

From my research, I can tell you that every container house I investigated that's currently up for sale has held its value very well. In most cases, the owner would be able to sell it and make a profit.

Clever Use of Space

I firmly believe that necessity is the mother of invention, and I love the way container houses have disrupted the way we think about space.

Most people would look at a 40ft container and wonder how they could possibly create a real living space for two people and their child. An innovative person looks beyond the restrictions and finds the solutions.

This innovative spirit is reflected in an article titled *Inside a Stylish Shipping Container Home for a Family of Three* (2019).

The article focuses on Kimberley Andrews, her husband James Innes, and their daughter Nova. Their house is a 40ft container, stacked on top of two 20ft containers from where they run their business.

There is no bedroom to be found. On the one side of the container is a shower and toilet, on the other side the dining room. In between is the entry and the kitchen.

It's only once you start looking closer that you notice the smart use of space. The couch is slightly elevated, but there's still more than enough room left over. The double bed pulls out underneath the couch, but that's not the only trick. On either side of the double bed, there are drawers. These extend out to form benches. Lift their lids up and you'll find the couple's clothes. From another storage space, they remove a small fold-up table, and presto—a dining room.

On the outside, there's a deck with a small bath. When the weather is right, the couple can take their baths outside. When it's not, they use the shower inside. The bath also doubles as a small play pool for their daughter.

This $100,000 house (all-inclusive) is a magnificent achievement and one I believe is already being replicated by furniture companies across the globe, not just as a result of container houses, but also because apartments simply aren't being built as big as they once were.

Furniture Makers Catching On

If you Google "furniture for tiny houses" you won't be disappointed. Large retailers are now getting in on the action, which is nice to see. I like the disruption and the clever thinking that drives people toward designing new ideas.

There are many examples, but I shall only name a few of my favorites, starting with the Drop-Leaf Table. Unlike most tables, which have four legs and a large piece of wood in the middle, Drop-Leaf Tables fold open to form a large-enough platform to eat on. They also fold flat to easily store beneath a bed or against the wall and out of the way.

I also enjoy folding furniture mounted to walls. These things replace so many pieces of furniture that would normally clutter a home. A great example is a working desk. When it's folded, the desk is flat against the wall. You could even mount a nice picture on the bottom, so it's a nice design feature when not in use. When you need it, you simply unlatch it and it creates a large working space.

Along the same lines, but much bigger, we find wall beds. These require you to give up a foot or two of the wall on the inside, but it clears up massive amounts of floor space. On the flip side, you can install almost anything on the other side of the bed. An extra desk, some bookshelves, a television, and so forth.

We touched on smart drawers earlier, but it's worth mentioning again. For decades now the base of a bed has been just that. When you look at the amount of storage space underneath, it's actually shocking that nobody has thought of utilizing it before. These bases come in multiple shapes and sizes. You can get bases with drawers that pull out, perfect for clothes, towels, DVDs, books, or anything else that size. You can also get a bed with a base that lifts up completely, allowing you to store much larger items, such as fold-up bikes, or Drop-Leaf Tables.

As far as I am concerned, you can look at every possible surface or feature as an additional storage space. When you have two containers stacked on top of each other, the interior is obviously going to have a staircase. It can be just that, or you can use each stair as a storage space.

Tiny house living forces us to take a closer look at the space we have available, and what we can do with it.

How To Decorate a Container House

Let's start with the basics first.

If you look at the majority of interior photographs of container houses, you'll note that 99% of them are decorated with lighter shades of wood or paint.

Certain colors just make a room feel bigger, and it makes even more of an impact if you contrast it with another color. It all comes down to light, you see. Dark colors have a tendency to absorb light, which makes a room feel smaller. Lighter walls are more reflective, creating the illusion of space and air.

While we're on the topic of air, here's another tip that is commonly used in moderate climates. It is possible to completely remove a container's sidewalls and replace them with either glass or sliding doors. This, by itself, creates the illusion of air and space, but we can take it a step further than that. You can build a veranda on one or both sides of the container and open the sliding door completely.

This is easily achievable if you're using a slab as a foundation. Instead of pouring the foundation a few inches wider than the shipping container, pour it larger on what will be the sides of the container. There will be a step between the container and the foundation, but you can always install an elevated wooden platform. You could even decorate the exterior platform the same way as the interior for added effect.

As for decorating the container house with furniture, don't get more than you need. Place function ahead of style at all times. Take into account how many people will live there, and buy only for them.

When picking furniture, keep an eye out for double-duty items. A bed with storage space in the platform is a perfect example. A sleeper couch in the living room is another.

This can make the interior of a house seem rather dreary, but instead of adding your own unique personality via large pieces of furniture, rather do so with small touches. I'm talking about small art pieces, paintings, candles, plants, and photographs. Get the big stuff in place, and leave the overall feel to the smaller items. You'll be surprised how much of an impact a well-placed coffee table book can have in a tiny house.

The Downsides

It wouldn't be fair to write an entire book about shipping container homes and not look at some of the main concerns people have raised over the years.

First and foremost, we have the environmental argument. When you buy a new shipping container to build a house, there's no recycling involved. To build a new container also requires more steel than is used to build the average normal house, which means you actually use more resources (Hunter, 2020).

It's a valid point, and one to keep in mind if you're building a container house because of how environmentally friendly it is. To ensure you use as little resources as possible, you'll need to shop for a used container. If going green is the main consideration, there are loads of other things to consider along the way, such as connecting to utilities and where you decide to place it. We live in an age where the technology is available, which means at the end of the build there's a very real possibility that the foundation will be the only negative impact you have on the environment. The methods are out there, you just need to do the research.

The second criticism is aimed at structural rigidity and insulation. Like I've said before in this book, if you're not an expert in building materials, you shouldn't remove large chunks of a container. The structure will be compromised, which is why you need to seek expert advice when doing so. Insulation is also a tricky problem, mostly due to the limited space on the inside. You only have 8ft to work with, so you don't necessarily want to limit the space even further by fitting thick insulation. The solution is to insulate on the outside, but then you lose that iconic shipping container look. I don't really see this as a problem. It's more of a practical question. If you live in an area with a moderate climate, it's not a problem. If you don't, you'll have to insulate. You either have the option of losing more space on the inside or losing the looks on the outside. I'll leave that for you to decide.

There are also some safety concerns when it comes to used containers. Because they were never built for humans to live in, some of the materials used on the inside may not be that good for your health. During its time at sea, that container might also have been used to transport something unsafe. It's a valid point, which is why I pointed out the need to be careful when shopping for a container. Containers that were built to transport hazardous materials are built differently, and you need to stay far away from them.

And as for the hazardous materials, you simply need to clean that container out as thoroughly as possible. If there is lead-based paint on the inside, you need to sand it down safely and replace it with something more appropriate.

The final point mentioned in many articles is the red tape. Yes, there is a lot of it, but if you use the advice that I gave in chapter 2, you should be fine.

Conclusion

At the time of writing, the world is already on its way toward recovering from the pandemic, at least from a health point of view.

However, the devastating effects of this pandemic on the economy will likely be with us for many years to come. It's during times like these that many are looking for more affordable housing options, and shipping container homes provide the perfect solution.

But to only focus on shipping container houses within the context of the pandemic would be a disservice to the ingenuity behind it.

Just think about it. What started as a standardized shipping system has ended up as a revolutionary way to build a new house for much cheaper than ever before.

Shipping container houses are strong, flexible, and modular. They allow the owner to be part of the creative process and express themselves through their home. Up until now, that's a luxury that has only been afforded to the rich.

To many, the size may seem like too much of a sacrifice, but it can be a good thing for many reasons. During my time in a tiny house, I was struck by how little I actually needed to get by. A container house doesn't just have an effect on your living situation, but it changes the way you see the world as well. Minimalism is all the rage right now, and I also think it's more than just a mere trend.

The behavior of the next generation of buyers suggests that it will be the way we that many of us live in the future. You only buy what you need, and you only take up as much space as you need. This is not only good for the soul but good for your wallet and good for the environment.

The rest of the world is catching on as well. We can see this in the mass production of ready-made shipping container homes and the furniture to go along with them.

Yes, there are still many things standing in the way, but I think it will get easier the more popular shipping container houses get. At the moment there's still much confusion around the categorization of container houses and building standards, but the more people that buy them, the quicker the government will catch on and find ways to make the process smoother.

If nothing else, I hope this book has encouraged you to take a closer look at shipping container houses, even if you just want one as a holiday home.

It's a fascinating building method, and one I'm 100% convinced we'll see more often in the very near future.

References

Bartash, J. (2020, August 7). *The U.S. has only regained 42% of the 22 million jobs lost in the pandemic. Here's where they are.* MarketWatch. https://www.marketwatch.com/story/restaurants-and-retailers-have-regained-the-most-jobs-since-the-coronavirus-crisis-but-theres-a-catch-2020-08-07

Butler, P. (2019, August 23). *"They just dump you here": the homeless families living in shipping containers.* The Guardian. https://www.theguardian.com/society/2019/aug/23/they-just-dump-you-here-the-homeless-families-living-in-shipping-containers

CSI opportunities for SA businesses: Shipping container crèches, schools and libraries. (2019, May 13). Big Box Containers. https://www.bigboxcontainers.co.za/blog/csi-opportunities-sa-businesses-shipping-container-creches-schools-libraries

Davis, M. & Perino, D. (2020, April 10). *Here's the typical home price in every state — and what you can actually get for that money.* Business Insider. https://www.businessinsider.com/average-home-prices-in-every-state-washington-dc-2019-6?IR=T

Hunter, L. (2018, November 29). *Container homes - pros, cons & cost comparison.* Rise. https://www.buildwithrise.com/stories/container-homes-are-exactly-what-they-sound-like-homes

Inside a stylish shipping container home for a family of three. (2019, September 16). Www.Homestolove.Co.Nz. https://www.homestolove.co.nz/real-homes/home-tours/inside-stylish-shipping-container-home

ISO containers selection guide | Engineering360. (n.d.). Www.Globalspec.Com. Retrieved September 25, 2020, from https://www.globalspec.com/learnmore/material_handling_packaging_equipment/material_handling_equipment/iso_containers#:~:text=The%20standard%20used%20to%20identify

Kirby, N. (2018, February 6). *What's really right? Corporate Social Responsibility as a legal obligation in South Africa - Werksmans.* Werksmans. https://www.werksmans.com/legal-updates-and-opinions/whats-really-right-corporate-social-responsibility-as-a-legal-obligation-in-south-africa/

Pedersen, C. L., Meyer, K., & Ritter, T. (2020, April 12). *The coronavirus crisis: A catalyst for entrepreneurship.* The Conversation. https://theconversation.com/the-coronavirus-crisis-a-catalyst-for-entrepreneurship-135005

Popcorn, F. (2020). Faith Popcorn's BrainReserve - The Future of Homes Report - Page 1. Zine.Faithpopcorn.Com. https://zine.faithpopcorn.com/future-of-homes/page/1

Shipping container history: Boxes to buildings. (2020, May 11). Discover Containers. https://www.discovercontainers.com/a-complete-history-of-the-shipping-container/

Shipping container home foundations 101 - Discover Containers. (2015, September 3). Discover Containers. https://www.discovercontainers.com/shipping-container-home-foundation-types/

Shipping container zoning, permits, and building codes. (2019, August 27). Discover Containers. https://www.discovercontainers.com/shipping-container-zoning-permits-and-building-codes-which-states-allow-them/

2020 cost to build a house | New home construction cost (per sq ft). (2020). HomeGuide. https://homeguide.com/costs/cost-to-build-a-house

Used container grading and certification - CSI Containers. (n.d.). CSI Container Services International. Retrieved September 22, 2020, from https://www.csiu.co/used_container_grading_certification

www.ingramcontent.com/pod-product-compliance
Lightning Source LLC
LaVergne TN
LVHW021739060526
838200LV00052B/3360